First Publication Date: February 2020
ISBN: 978-81-939295-7-5
₹300 | US $9.99 | £7.99
Originally Published in Paperback
Cover Design: Linda Ashok

Manufactured in India, published & funded
by RLFPA Editions (OPC) Pvt Ltd.

BRASS NECK

*A collection of poetry on the genesis of queerness, sexual deviance,
and alpha sexual exposure*

CONTENTS

INTRODUCTION

By Ilya Kaminsky

Reading this Brass Neck, one thinks of Whitman's passion for the body and insistence that one's on the connection of all of our bodies, our voices, our pain and pleasure.

Of course, Whitman wasn't the first to give us the poetics of the body. The poems of this book make one think of Sappho and Catullus as much as they do of Whitman. And, yet, it is Walt's "barbaric yawp on the rooftops of the world" that echoes so much into our own era. One thinks of Orhan Veli of Turkey and Anna Swir of Poland, Israel's Yona Wollach and many others who have responded to his call. The author of Brass Neck responds as well. There is a large embrace of erotic and ecstatic impulses in this work. There are poems of early desire. They are sweet in their innocence:

Grandma

Grandma says boys can smell the scent of a pantyless vagina a gush of wind away.
i open my legs and allow the breeze to carry me away.

There are also poems of almost Sapphic longing:

women smell like flowers
i am drawn to flowers

women taste like fruits
i love strawberry bubblegum

a new girl just boarded my bus
i want her juice on my tongue.

The discovery of one's sensuality here is also Sapphic:

Touching Skin

a little girl touches skin under a wooden desk
two little girls touch skin under a wooden desk
three little girls touch skin under a wooden table
a class of little girls touch skin under
or on top of whatever the fuck they can find.
little girls touch skin. period.

The longing in such poems can be almost folkloric:

Temple

"your body is a temple"

temples are built for worship, rukie
show me a temple that never held worshippers
— that never held men.

men are worshippers
men bring praise
they bring promises,
harvest,
milk.

open your temple for worship.

Then, there is a harsher humor, and yet it still possesses a kind of innocence of learning the other's body, and one's own desire:

he said, "let me stick it in the back once"
three weeks later
i said, "let me stick it in the back once"

And there are poems that give us a fable of real-life tragedy, of a destroyed childhood, broken family:

Glue

protect your home
stick glue on your lips
and let your gaze wander
when your husband
puts a baby into your daughter.

There are other such tragic, terrifying lines in this book. Cousins do to cousins what people should never do to one another. The real terror is opened up to us in just a few lines. Where might this poet go from such knowledge? One wonders. How to console something that's so inconsolable?

At that point, one is compelled to find in this work a tonal shift that employs irony to show us what is learned after experience, what is the wisdom of this broken world:

Proving Manhood 101

"real men show no weakness"

take a girl,
smother her with your big man hand

Perhaps this irony is a way of coping with pain. One is also competed to see that despite this tragic knowledge, the poet still possesses tenderness for the body, even if its one's own:

An Act of Love

Sometimes I kiss myself. I put my arm forward, plant my big bold lips on my skin and suck it in. Even the after sound gets sucked into my stomach. I'm curious about how my skin feels; how this body tastes.

This too, is an act of love.

By the end, one learns that if there is a Whitmanic impulse in this book, it is the kind of impulse that is transformed by pain of experience, a kind that reminds one of Lucille Clifton's large, generous, consoling voice yet also one that comes in glimpses of experience after a great pain. Epigrammatic quality here is crucial, it is what moves these poems forward, allowing for the wider range of experience, allowing the sensual world also become one of emotional intelligence. "Home is the chaos / where you feel / most alive," this poet tells us. One is moved by the terrible pain and utter betrayal of girlhood in that many poems in this book showcase. And, at the same time, one is also surprised and compelled by the author's uplift, by the unexpected tonalities, humor. In both of these realms the sensuality and freshness of perspective are striking.

This is a poet to watch. ✦

Poems by

Victoria Naa Takia Nunoo

Winner of

RL POETRY AWARD 2018

Selected by

ILYA KAMINSKY

TOUCHING SKIN

a little girl touches skin under a wooden desk
two little girls touch skin under a wooden desk
three little girls touch skin under a wooden table
a class of little girls touch skin under
or on top of whatever the fuck they can find.
little girls touch skin. period

CONCRETE WALLS

whatever it is you desire
tell it inside a locked room
when you have heard the keys turn

tell it inside concrete walls
with their pores sealed with paint

tell it to the darkness
that no one else can see

tell it with no voice
bearing in mind that
if you speak too loud
day will hear you
and night may never come again

tell it beside square walls
echoing with the sound of water

tell it to a brother
with his eyes glazed with sleep

tell it with a bar of soap
and a rub.

TOWER OF WOMEN

night clubs and neon lights
strangers and booze
body chemistry

"boys are pain"

tonight women tower
on each other's bodies.

BEHIND NARROW HOUSES

your oldest cousin looks at you
like ripe *salo mangoes*
you are only nine
but,
"you have the body of a sixteen year old"
behind narrow houses,
and broken windows with torn mosquito nets,
are your playground.
hide and seek,
police and thief,
guns loaded with
imaginary bullets start firing
only the guns are his fingers
and his aim, your vagina.

CREEPY PLEASURES

mother
father
brothers
sisters
uncles
aunties
first cousin
second cousin
third cousin
one bathroom
one door
one spectacular view beneath
prostrate,
as soon as you hear water hit,
bush land,
bare land,
watermelon breasts,
pawpaw breasts,
onion breasts,
orange seed breasts,
choose your choice,
feast your eyes,
come.

TEMPLE

"your body is a temple"

temples are built for worship, rukie
show me a temple that never held worshippers
– that never held men.

men are worshippers
men bring praise
they bring promises,
harvest,
milk.

open your temple for worship.

THE REAR

he said, "*let me stick it in the back once*"
three weeks later
i said, "*let me stick it in the back once*"

AN ACT OF LOVE

Sometimes I kiss myself. I put my arm forward, plant my big bold lips on my skin and suck it in. Even the after sound gets sucked into my stomach. I'm curious about how my skin feels; how this body tastes.

This too, is an act of love.

OF ALL THINGS FRUITY

women smell like flowers
i am drawn to flowers

women taste like fruits
i love strawberry bubblegum

a new girl just boarded my bus
i want her juice on my tongue.

GRANDMA

Grandma says boys can smell the scent of a pantyless vagina a gush of wind away.

I open my legs and allow the breeze to carry me away.

BOARDING SCHOOL

from where you lay,
teenage bodies stretch out before you.
in the darkness your mind,
where fear resides,
you see a mass burial;
an army of young sleeping souls.
narrow wood,
thin student mattresses,
white linen,
stiff bodies.
"top beds are for first years only,
but you can share my bed when
the darkness comes",
you remember Sister Veronica say.

SON RISE

find your mother's baby
every morning
and watch that son rise
from his groin.

PROVING MANHOOD 101

"real men show no weakness"

take a girl,
smother her with your big man hand
part her *Jordan* with your strong man knees
spread yourself,
like a burning bush fire on her
scorch her with your heat
repeat as needed.

GLUE

protect your home
stick glue on your lips
and let your gaze wander
when your husband
puts a baby into your daughter.

OUTIE NAVEL

mother wears no panties before going to bed
every night she lifts her silk nightie up
and climbs on top of father's stomach
his outie navel looks even bigger and longer at night
Jojo in fourth grade at school has an outie navel
i should ask him if his grow longer at night too.

THE ESCAPE

if the world is ours,
we should totally
fuck on it.

REENACTING A PAST

does a piece of furniture
ever remind you of someone?
sounds so loud in your ear
you black out completely.
now all you want to do
is to situate every one
of your lovers there
do they know
you're reenacting a past?

CUTTING CARROTS

[sees a teensy-weensy carrot]

throwback to your first finger job
that orgasm came faster than you
could hear yourself moan

men have come and gone
only their fingers stayed.

the man you're with now
doesn't know his fingers
are his best bet.

RAGE SEX

rage sex is your favorite
for you, pain, somehow,
is the most indication of reality.

STEAMY MOTION

making love is such work
even saying the phrase is exhausting
let's fuck
that's more like it.
it rolls off the tongue easily
and sets steamy motion.

A GIRL CALLED RUKIE

when ken returned from school
a failed seminarian,
he said he had found other ways'
to serve God.

her name was rukie.

MAN-STORIES

cruel men live in the lips of my bestfriend
their names and stories
are carved into the walls of her throat
i want to move closer to her
hold her tight face in my hands
and suck those wretched men out
instead, i make up man-stories of my own.

LOVE

love has no one colour
or one face
or one body
or one gender

love is who or what projects
the best version of you.

MORE THAN JUST MEMORIES

i am growing myself
in every place
seeking love
even in my own kind
and hoping to harvest
more than just memories.

GRAVEYARDS OF SILENCE

On these streets
two choices await you:

i
cut your tongue off

ii
or have a ball of fire placed on it

eitherways, our bodies
are meant to be graveyards of silence.

SORDID AFFAIR

hold your sacrifice
close to your chest
till he synchronises
with your breathing
this is the light
you traded for darkness.

CLOSET

how much more of the burns can you take
before you free your soul?

soon, this closet won't hold.

MOB (IN) JUSTICE

i have come here to love
i have not come here to burn.

NOTHING LIKE MY MOTHER

i

when i was twelve i stoned the tenant's louvre and
pressed myself to his wall such that he didn't see me
when he looked out. then i watched to see the deep
crack in the ugly glassy thing before scurrying away.

ii

i searched my mother's face when she came home.
she wore disappointment like her favorite dress,
mumbled curses under her breath, and refused to talk
to father that night.
i heard her say to him the morning after, "glass is so
expensive and we barely have enough to eat. maybe
we should go back to using wooden windows. they
are less costly and can easily be replaced when
broken. and they are more secure. intruders cannot
see through wood."

iii

that afternoon, i saw my papa replace the tenant's
glass window with a wooden one. he worked hard
and whistled loud. cracked smiles formed at the sides
of his mouth. "when you grow up", he said to me,
"marry a woman who has a head and a heart like your
mother."

i knew i would grow up to want a woman who was
nothing like my mother.

WHEN THE SUNSHINE COMES

they will come
they will come with their cloak
of darkness and try to wrap it around you.

when they do,
wait for the sunshine;
the light that glows
on your skin and scars alike,
and teaches you to love all things
equally.

BURNT HOPE

the streets are reeking
of burnt hope
mouths are aiming guns
and firing bullets

they do not understand
the language of our bodies
or the song in our hearts.

BODY PARTS

who is to tell
which parts
of our bodies
we are to love with?

LOVING GOD

the closest i've come to loving God
is loving myself.

DESIRE

desire sits on your tongue like fire
and it moves through your whole body
there's chemistry in the air;
in the way she spreads herself next to you
is she a door longing to be opened?
waiting to be held?

SEVENTEEN

the first time i wanted to be loved, i was sixteen. i snuck into adelaide's beauty shop and shaved half my eyebrows away to look more like a woman. the second time i wanted to be loved, i was seventeen. i'd miss several lectures to play tongues with a boy in whose room i'd later wake up in with drums to my head and a blood bath inside my thighs. the third time i wanted to be loved, i situated my own vagina and poked myself till my eyes rolled to the back and my lips moistened with pleasure. i was still seventeen.

FIST LOVE

i
you spend several hours
huddled behind your family's only leather couch.
and with every tear-filled moan,
you sink another nail into the black material.
many half moons stare back at you.

ii
your mother says it is an act of love;
that father has too much love for her
the excess spills into his fist.

iii
thirteen years on,
you're staring at a black eye in front of
a bathroom mirror.
this is an act of love;
your face breaks into a painful smile.

SOCIETY

society is one person before it becomes people.
one opinion before it becomes common opinion.

LOVE BITES

get high on electric music
body connect on fine lyrics,
literature and booze
binge-watch netflix
fuck each other's brains out
and when you forget
how good this feels
the reminders are there on your neck.

WHAT IT MEANS TO HAVE AN ANGRY BODY

the first time i learnt that a body could be angry,
i had passed through three stages of emotions;
fear, confusion and pain. i had cursed at the darkness and shelter
it gave perpetrators of crime.
pain shot through me as he took and took until my body grew
angry; so angry that it wouldn't feel anything anymore.

ANOTHER KIND OF HOME

at other times
home is in the chaos

where you feel
most alive.

TEENAGE BODIES

i
the morning after compulsory church service
you gather around the illegal call center in your white frocks and
blue cardigans and take turns calling random network help lines
– a prayer on your lips that a male voice answers.

ii
a male voice fills your ears. he says his name is augustine, andhe
sounds like malt mixed with evaporated milk. your teenage body
catches fire and you immediately attempt a lighter accent.

DIPO

bukie's father refused to let his daughter roam the streets half
naked as an initiation into womanhood,
even though her mother had fought against him saying, *"it is the
only way to keep girls from being promiscuous."*

bukie is sneaking out of school today in mufti to meet her town
boyfriend.

sometimes i wonder if she would have turned out differently had
she undergone her puberty rites.

QUACK DOCTOR

you ran away from home at sixteen with a swollen
abdomen and sore black nipples. the night women
whispered the location of "the doctor" to you.
with your legs high above your head, the man in
filthy white overalls whistled through his gap as he
worked his tools inside you. three hours later, you
were gripping the seat in front of you and letting
out painful moans every time your ramshackle bus
landed in a pothole.

FIREWORKS

you can equate the feeling of touching yourself till your body explodes and your juices erupt to the exciting blast of fireworks on new year's eve, especially with the countdown.

FREE THERAPY

the first guy you refused to have sex with locked
you in a room and threatened to leave with the
keys.

the second guy held you down and grinded you –
metals belts and hard zips – till your vagina felt
like the aftermath of an earthquake.

the third guy said you had psychological
problems and needed help or you'd never be able
to love a man, physically.

the moving ad at the bottom of your tv screen
says there's free therapy for young women who
have suffered trauma or sexual abuse. the toll
free number to call slowly glides by.

WHO THEY'D RATHER YOU BE

anger is a resident feeling
when your only true-self
is unacceptable to society.

SOMETHING IS HAPPENING TO MOTHER AT NIGHT

last night you asked your cousin about the noises
mother makes at night and the gallons of water
she drinks after. you watched him laugh; the hole
in his left cheek more prominent than the right's.
if you promised you'd leave your bedroom door
open he said, he'd do you one better by showing
you how the noises come about.

BLACK SEX TOURISTS

with the bridges came new resorts, and with the new resorts came the white men; some with their families, but most with just money for adventure. coconut oil was costly during the holiday season because the white men without families liked to smell it on our bodies and hair, and would pay twice as much for it. when night came, we would drink pots of freshly brewed palm wine, cheer them on with our native songs, as they showed off their offbeat dancing, and then go with them to their rented rooms, where our brassieres became safes for foreign currency.

BEING INCAPABLE OF LOVE

the worst ever isn't loving one's own kind
it is being incapable of any kind of love.

WHY YOU WOULDN'T COME OUT

i understand.

in a world of intolerance, sometimes the safest
place to be is within yourself.

9 788819 392957 5